SHERLOCK HOLMES SHORT STORIES

When we think of a detective, we think first of Sherlock Holmes. Even now, a hundred years after the first story about him, he is still the greatest detective of all. Tourists still go to Baker Street, in London, to see the place where he had his apartment. There are films about him and pictures of him—we all know what he looked like and we all know what kind of clothes he wore.

And yet he never existed. The stories about him are just stories. So, why do we remember him?

It is because he loves catching criminals. Sherlock Holmes chases the criminal as a hunter chases a fox. He is a bloodhound, a police dog, with his nose to the ground—following the criminal to the end of the world. The criminal may try to hide—but when Sherlock Holmes has started the chase, we know that he will finish it with a "kill."

OXFORD BOOKWORMS LIBRARY

Crime & Mystery

Sherlock Holmes Short Stories

Stage 2 (700 headwords)

Series Editor: Jennifer Bassett
Founder Editor: Tricia Hedge
Activities Editors: Jennifer Bassett and Alison Baxter

American Edition: Daphne Mackey, University of Washington

SIR AUTHUR CONAN DOYLE

Sherlock Holmes Short Stories

Retold by
Clare West

OXFORD UNIVERSITY PRESS

OXFORD
UNIVERSITY PRESS

Great Clarendon Street, Oxford OX2 6DP

Oxford University Press is a department of the University of Oxford.
It furthers the University's objective of excellence in research, scholarship,
and education by publishing worldwide in

Oxford New York

Auckland Cape Town Dar es Salaam Hong Kong Karachi
Kuala Lumpur Madrid Melbourne Mexico City Nairobi
New Delhi Shanghai Taipei Toronto

With offices in

Argentina Austria Brazil Chile Czech Republic France Greece
Guatemala Hungary Italy Japan Poland Portugal Singapore
South Korea Switzerland Thailand Turkey Ukraine Vietnam

OXFORD and OXFORD ENGLISH are registered trade marks of
Oxford University Press in the UK and in certain other countries

First published in Oxford Bookworms 1989

6 8 10 9 7 5

ISBN 978 0 19 423751 2

Printed in China

ACKNOWLEDGMENTS

*The publishers would like to thank the following for their permission
to reproduce illustrations*: Mary Evans Picture Library
Illustration on p7 by: Paul Margiotta

CONTENTS

The Speckled Band

1

Helen's Story

At the time of this story, I was still living at my friend Sherlock Holmes's apartment in Baker Street in London. Very early one morning, a young woman, dressed in black, came to see us. She looked tired and unhappy, and her face was very white. "I'm afraid! Afraid of death, Mr. Holmes!" she cried. "Please help me! I'm not thirty yet and look at my gray hair! I'm so afraid!"

Very early one morning, a young woman, dressed in black, came to see us.

"Just sit down and tell us your story," said Holmes kindly.

"My name is Helen Stoner," she began, "and I live with my stepfather, Dr. Grimesby Roylott, near a village in the country. His family was once very rich, but they had no money when my stepfather was born. So he studied to be a doctor and went out to India. He met and married my mother there, when my sister Julia and I were very young. Our father was dead, you see."

"Your mother had some money, perhaps?" asked Sherlock Holmes.

"Oh yes, mother had a lot of money, so my stepfather wasn't poor any more."

"Tell me more about him, Miss Stoner," said Holmes.

"Well, he's a violent man. In India he once got angry with his Indian servant and killed him! He had to go to prison because of that, and then we all came back to England. Mother died in an accident eight years ago. So my stepfather got all her money, but if Julia or I marry, he has to pay us £250 every year."

"And now you live with him in the country," said Holmes.

"Yes, but he stays at home and never sees anybody, Mr. Holmes!" answered Helen Stoner. "He's more and more violent now, and sometimes has fights with the people from the village. Everybody's afraid of him now, and they run away when they see him. And they're also afraid of his Indian wild animals, which run freely around the garden. A friend sends them to him from India. And the animals are not the only wild things in the garden; there are also gypsies. My stepfather likes these wild people, and they can come and go where they like. Poor Julia and I had very unhappy lives. We had no servants. They always left because they were afraid of my stepfather, and we had to do all the work in the house. Julia was only thirty when she died, and her hair was already gray, like my hair now."

"When did she die?" asked Sherlock Holmes.

"She died two years ago, and that's why I'm here. We never met anybody in the country, but sometimes we visited some of my family who live near London. There Julia met a young man who asked to marry her. My stepfather agreed, but soon after this she died." Miss Stoner put her hand over her eyes and cried for a minute.

Sherlock Holmes was listening with his eyes closed, but now he opened them and looked at Helen Stoner.

"Tell me everything about her death," he said.

"I can remember it all very well. It was a terrible time!" she answered. "Our three bedrooms are all downstairs. First there is my stepfather's room. Julia's room is next to his, and my room is next to Julia's. The rooms all have windows on the garden side of the house and doors which open into the corridor. One evening our stepfather was smoking his strong Indian cigarettes in his room. Julia couldn't sleep because she could smell them in her room, so she came into my room to talk to me. Before she went back to bed, she said to me, 'Helen, have you ever heard a whistle in the middle of the night?'

"I was surprised. 'No,' I said.

" 'It's strange,' she said. 'Sometimes I hear a whistle, but I don't know where it comes from. Why don't you hear it?'

"I laughed and said, 'I sleep better than you do.' So Julia went to her room and locked the door after her."

"Why did you lock your doors?" asked Sherlock Holmes.

"We were afraid of the wild animals and the gypsies," she answered.

"Please go on," said Holmes.

"I couldn't sleep that night. It was a very stormy night, with a lot of wind and rain. Suddenly I heard a woman's scream. It was my sister's voice. I ran into the corridor, and just then I heard a whistle and a minute later the sound of falling metal. I didn't know what it was. I ran to my sister's door. She opened it and fell to the ground. Her face was white and afraid, and she was crying, 'Help me, help me, Helen. I'm ill. I'm dying!' I put my arms around her, and she cried out in a terrible voice: 'Helen! Oh my God, Helen! It was the band! The speckled band!' She wanted to say more, but she couldn't. I called my stepfather, who tried to

"My sister's face was white and afraid."

help her, but we could do nothing. And so my dear, dear sister died."

"Are you sure about the whistle and the sound of falling metal?" asked Holmes.

"I think so," answered Helen. "But it was a very wild, stormy night. Perhaps I made a mistake. The police couldn't understand why my sister died. Her door was locked, and nobody could get into her room. They didn't find any poison in her body. And what was 'the speckled band'? Gypsies wear something like that around their necks. I think she died because she was so afraid, but I don't know what she was afraid of. Perhaps it was the gypsies. What do you think, Mr. Holmes?"

Holmes thought for a minute. "Hmm," he said. "That is a difficult question. But please go on."

"That was two years ago," Helen Stoner said. "I have been very lonely without my sister, but a month ago a dear friend asked me to marry him. My stepfather has agreed, and so we're going to marry soon. But two days ago I had to move to my sister's old bedroom, because some men are mending my bedroom wall, and last night I heard that whistle again! I ran out of the house immediately and came to London to ask for your help. Please help me, Mr. Holmes! I don't want to die like Julia!"

"We must move fast," said Holmes. "If we go to your house today, can we look at these rooms? But your stepfather must not know."

"He's in London today, so he won't see you. Oh thank you, Mr. Holmes, I feel better already."

2

Holmes and Watson Visit the House

Holmes went out for the morning, but he came back at lunch-time. We then went by train into the country and took a taxi to Dr. Roylott's house. "You see," said Holmes to me, "our dangerous friend Roylott needs the girls' money because he only has £750 a year from his dead wife. I found that out this morning. But the

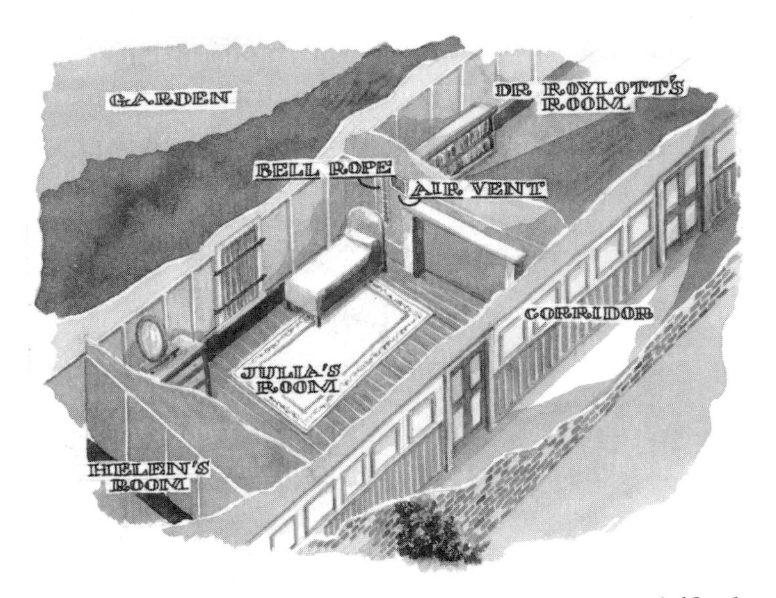

gypsies, the whistle, the band—they are more difficult to understand, but I think I have an answer."

When we arrived, Helen Stoner showed us the three bedrooms. We saw her room first.

"Why are they mending your bedroom wall?" asked Holmes. "There's nothing wrong with it."

"You're right," she said. "I think it was a plan to move me into my sister's room."

"Yes," said Holmes. We went into Julia's room, and Holmes looked at the windows carefully.

"Nobody could come in from outside," he said. Then he looked around the room. "Why is that bell rope there, just over the bed?"

"My stepfather put it there two years ago. It's for calling a servant, but Julia and I never used it because we didn't have any servants. He also put in that air vent on the wall between his room and this one."

Holmes pulled the rope. "But it doesn't work," he said. "How strange! And it's just over the air vent. That also is interesting. Why have an air vent on an inside wall? Air vents are usually on outside walls."

Then we went into Dr. Roylott's room. Holmes saw a large metal box near the wall.

"My stepfather keeps business papers in there," said Helen.

"Does he keep a cat in there too?" asked Holmes. "Look!" There was some milk on a plate on top of the

"Does your stepfather keep a cat in there too?" asked Holmes.

box. "Now, Miss Stoner," he said, "I think your life is in danger. Tonight my friend Watson and I must spend the night in your sister's room, where you are sleeping at the moment."

Helen Stoner and I looked at him in surprise.

"Yes, we must," he went on. "We'll take a room in a hotel in the village. When your stepfather goes to bed, put a light in your sister's bedroom window and leave it open. Then go into your old room, and we'll get into your sister's room through the window. We'll wait for the sound of the whistle and the falling metal."

"How did my sister die, Mr. Holmes? Do you know?

"Now goodbye, Miss Stoner, and don't be afraid," said Holmes.

Please tell me!" said Helen. She put her hand on Sherlock Holmes's arm.

"I must find out more before I tell you, Miss Stoner. Now goodbye, and don't be afraid," replied Sherlock Holmes.

We walked to the village, and Holmes said to me, "Tonight will be dangerous, Watson. Roylott is a very violent man."

"But if I can help, Holmes, I'll come with you," I said.

"Thank you, Watson. I'll need your help. Did you see the bell rope, and the air vent? I knew about the air vent before we came. Of course there is a hole between the two rooms. That explains why Helen's sister could smell Dr. Roylott's cigarette."

"My dear Holmes! How clever of you!" I cried.

"And did you see the bed? It's fixed to the floor. *She can't move it.* It has to stay under the rope, which is near the air vent."

"Holmes!" I cried. "I begin to understand! What a terrible crime!"

"Yes, this doctor is a very clever man. But we can stop him, I think, Watson."

3

Death in the Night

That night we went back to the house. When we saw Helen Stoner's light, Holmes and I got in quietly through the window. Then we waited silently in the middle bedroom in the dark. We waited for three hours and did not move. Suddenly we saw a light and heard a sound from Dr. Roylott's room. But nothing happened, and again we waited in the dark. Then there was another sound, a very quiet sound ... Immediately Holmes jumped up and hit the bell rope hard.

"Can you see it, Watson?" he shouted. But I saw nothing. There was a quiet whistle. We both looked up at the air vent, and suddenly we heard a terrible cry in the next room. Then the house was silent again.

Immediately Holmes jumped up and hit the bell rope hard.

Around his head was a strange, yellow speckled band. He was dead.

"What does it mean?" I asked. My voice was shaking.

"It's finished," answered Holmes. "Let's go and see."

We went into Dr. Roylott's room. The metal box was open. Roylott was sitting on a chair, and his eyes were fixed on the air vent. Around his head was a strange, yellow speckled band. He was dead.

"The band! The speckled band!" said Holmes very quietly. The band moved and began to turn its head. "Be careful, Watson! It's a snake, an Indian snake—and its poison can kill very quickly," Holmes cried. "Roylott died immediately. We must put the snake back in its box." Very, very carefully, Holmes took the snake and threw it into the metal box.

"But how did you know about the snake, Holmes?" I asked.

"At first, Watson, I thought that it was the gypsies. But then I understood. I thought that perhaps something came through the air vent, down the bell rope, and onto the bed. Then there was the milk—and of course, snakes drink milk. It was easy for the Doctor to get Indian animals. And because he was a doctor, he knew that this snake's poison is difficult to find in a dead body. So every night he put the snake through the air vent, and it went down the bell rope onto the bed. Of course, nobody must see the snake, so every night he whistled to call it back. The sound of metal falling was the door of the metal box, which was the snake's home. Perhaps the snake came through the air vent many times before it killed Julia. But in the end it killed her. And Helen, too, nearly died because of this snake.

"But tonight, when I hit the snake on the rope, it was angry and went back through the air vent. And so it killed the Doctor. I'm not sorry about that."

Soon after this Helen Stoner married her young man and tried to forget the terrible deaths of her sister and stepfather. But she never really forgot the speckled band.

A Scandal in Bohemia

1

The King's Mistake

For Sherlock Holmes, there was only one woman in the world. He did not love her because he never loved women. But after their meeting he never forgot her. Her name was Irene Adler.

One night in March I visited my old friend at his home in Baker Street. I was married by now, so I did not often see him.

"Come in, Watson," he said. "Sit down. I'm happy to see you, because I've got something to show you. What do you think of this? It arrived in the last mail delivery." It was a letter, with no date, name, or address. It said:

"Tonight someone will visit you to talk about some very secret business. You have helped other important people, and you can, we hope, help us. Be in your room at 7.45 p.m."

"The paper—what do you think about the paper?" asked Holmes.

I tried to think like Holmes. "It's expensive, so this person is rich. It's strange paper."

"Yes, it's not English. If you look at it in the light, you can see that it was made in Bohemia. And a German, I think, wrote the letter. Ah, here comes our man now."

We could hear the horses in the street.

"Shall I leave, Holmes?" I asked.

"No, no, I need your help. This will be interesting," my friend answered. There was a knock at the door.

"Come in!" called Holmes.

A tall, strong man came into the room. He was wearing expensive clothes and a mask over his face.

"You can call me Count von Kramm. I come from Bohemia," he said. "My business is most important. Before I tell you about it, do you agree to keep it a secret?"

"I do," we said together.

"A very important person, who belongs to a royal family, has sent me to ask for your help," he went on. "I wear a mask because nobody must know who that person is. I must explain how important this business is. If you cannot help, there will be difficulty and trouble for one of the most important families in Europe—and perhaps a very big scandal. I am talking about the famous House of Ormstein, Kings of Bohemia."

"I know, Your Majesty," said Holmes. He quietly smoked his cigarette.

The man jumped up from his chair. "What!" he cried. "How do you know who I am?" Then he pulled the mask off his face and threw it on the ground. "You are right. Why do I hide it? I am the King. I am Wilhelm von Ormstein, King of Bohemia. I came to see you

He was wearing expensive clothes and a mask.

myself because I could not ask another person to tell my story. It *must* be a secret. You understand?"

"Very well. Go on," said Holmes. He closed his eyes and listened.

"Five years ago I met a woman called Irene Adler. We ..."

"Ah," said Holmes, "Irene Adler, born in 1850, singer, lives in London, a very beautiful woman, I hear ..." He looked at the King. "You and she ... You loved her, for a while, and then left her. But before you left her, you wrote her some letters perhaps. And now you want to get these letters back."

"That's right."

"Did you marry her?"

"No."

"If she asks you for money and shows you the letters, you can say that you didn't write them."

"But Mr. Holmes, she also has my photograph."

"You can say that you didn't give her a photograph."

"We were both in the photograph."

"Oh dear. That was a mistake, Your Majesty."

"I know. I was stupid ... but I was very young!"

"You must get the photograph back. Can you steal it from her house?"

"I have tried five times, but my men couldn't find it. What can I do?"

Holmes laughed. "This is very interesting. What does she plan to do with the photograph?"

"Soon I am going to marry Clotilde Lothman von Saxe-Meningen, daughter of the King of Scandinavia. You know, of course, that we are two of the most important royal families in Europe. Clotilde will never marry me if she learns that I have been a … friend of Irene Adler. You do not know Irene Adler. She's a beautiful woman, but she can be as hard as a man. She was angry when I left her, and so she doesn't want me to marry another woman. I know that she will send this photograph to the Saxe-Meningen family, and then there will be a terrible scandal. We must find the photograph before she sends it!"

"I am sure that we will find it," said Holmes. "You are, of course, staying in London? I will write to you to tell you what happens. And, the money …?"

The King put a large heavy bag on the table. "I must have that photograph," he said. "There is one thousand pounds here. If you need more, you must ask at once. The money is not important."

"And the young woman's address?" asked Holmes.

"Briony Lodge, Serpentine Avenue, St. John's Wood, London."

"Good night, Your Majesty," said Holmes. "I hope to have some good news for you soon." The King left, and Holmes turned to me. "And good night, Watson. Please come back tomorrow at three o'clock in the afternoon."

2

A Servant Finds Out

When I arrived the next day, Holmes was not there, so I waited in his room. At four o'clock the door opened, and a very strange servant came in. He wore old, dirty clothes, and I had to look very hard before I saw that it was my old friend.

"Holmes!" I cried. "Where have you been?"

"I've had a very good day," he replied with a smile. "I've been outside Miss Irene Adler's house. Servants are always happy to talk, and so I have heard a lot about the young woman. For example, she has a good-looking man friend called Godfrey Norton, a lawyer, who often visits her. Now why? If he's her lawyer, perhaps she's already given him the photograph. But if he loves her, she won't show him the photograph."

"Most interesting, Holmes!" I said.

"While I was there, Mr. Norton himself suddenly arrived. I watched them through the windows. When he left, he jumped into a taxi. 'To the church of St. Monica, as fast as you can!' he shouted. Two minutes later Miss Adler ran out of her house, jumped into another taxi and called, 'To the church of St. Monica, quickly!' I couldn't miss this, Watson, so I jumped into a third taxi. When I arrived, I went into the church. Godfrey Norton looked around and saw me.

"And so I helped Godfrey Norton to marry Irene Adler."

'Thank God!' he shouted. 'Come here quickly!' 'Why?' I asked. 'Come on, man, we need you!' And so I helped Godfrey Norton to marry Irene Adler. They needed a witness, and a servant from the street was better than nobody."

"So she married him! What shall we do now?" I asked.

"Well, tonight, my dear Watson, I need your help. Will you do what I ask? Without questions?"

"Of course, Holmes, if you think that it's important," I answered.

"Later, we'll go to Briony Lodge. Irene Adler, or Irene Norton, will arrive home at seven o'clock, and she will ask me to go into the house. You must wait outside near the sitting-room window, and when it opens, watch me inside. When I hold up my hand, throw this thing into the room and shout 'Fire!' "

I took the small thing out of his hand. "What is it, Holmes?" I asked.

"It's a smoke stick. The room will very quickly be full of smoke. After that, wait for me at the corner of the street."

"Right, I'll do what you want," I said.

3

Fire!

That evening Holmes again wore different clothes, and a large, black hat. But it was not just the clothes that were different. He changed his face, his hair—everything. He was a different man.

We walked together to Serpentine Avenue. Outside the house there were a lot of people who were smoking, laughing, and talking. Holmes and I walked up and down in front of the house.

"You see," said Holmes to me, "I think she doesn't want her new husband to see the photograph. But where is it? At her bank? No. Women like to keep important things themselves. I'm sure it's in her house."

"But the King's men tried to find it!" I said.

"Yes, but they didn't know where to look!" said Holmes.

"But how will *you* know?" I asked.

"I won't look. She'll show me. She'll have to."

Just then a taxi arrived. One of the men in the street ran to open the door, then another man pushed him. Other men were also pushing and shouting, and a fight began. Irene Norton was in the middle of it, but Sherlock Holmes ran to help her. Then suddenly he fell to the ground with blood running down his face. Irene Norton hurried to her front door, but she looked back.

Then Holmes fell to the ground with blood running down his face.

"How kind of him to help me! Is the poor man hurt?" she called.

"He's dead," cried some voices.

"No, he's only hurt," cried others.

"Bring him into the sitting-room," she said.

Some people carried Holmes into the house. I waited outside the window and watched. I saw how beautiful Irene Norton was. Then Holmes put up his hand, and I threw the smoke stick into the room. Immediately the people in the street and in the house all began to shout "Fire!" very loudly. The house was full of smoke. I walked away, and ten minutes later Holmes came to meet me.

"Well done, Watson," he said.

"Have you got the photograph?" I asked.

"I know where it is. She showed me," he answered.

"But why did she show you?"

"It's easy," he said, and laughed. "You saw all those people in the street? I paid them to help us. It wasn't a real fight, and the blood wasn't real. When people shout 'Fire!', a woman runs to the most important

A young man hurried past us and said, "Good night, Mr. Sherlock Holmes."

thing in her house, her baby, her gold, or ... a photograph. Mrs. Norton ran to find her photograph, which is in a cupboard in the sitting-room. I saw it. But I did not take it. Tomorrow we will go to her house with the King. We'll go very early, before she gets up. The King himself can take the photograph from the cupboard. And then we'll go."

While Holmes was talking, we were walking home to Baker Street. When we arrived at my friend's house, a young man hurried past us and said, "Good night, Mr. Sherlock Holmes."

"I've heard that voice before," said Holmes to me. He looked down the street. "But who was it?"

4

A Photograph

The next day we went to Irene Norton's house with the King. An old servant opened the door. "Mr. Sherlock Holmes?" she asked and smiled.

"Yes," said my friend. He looked very surprised.

"Mrs. Irene Norton and her husband left England this morning. They will never come back to this country."

"What?" cried Holmes, his face white and angry.

"And what about the photograph?" cried the King.

We all hurried into the sitting-room. Holmes ran to the cupboard and opened it. Inside was a photograph, not of Irene Adler and the King, but of the beautiful Irene alone. There was also a letter for Sherlock Holmes. We all read it together.

> My dear Mr. Sherlock Holmes,
> You did it very well. I thought that it was a real fire and that you were just a kind old man. But after I opened the cupboard, I began to think. I knew about the famous Sherlock Holmes. I knew your address, and I knew that the King asked you to find the photograph. So I quickly dressed as a young man and followed you home to Baker Street. I wanted to find out if you really were Sherlock Holmes. I said "good night" to you outside your door!
>
> My husband and I have decided to leave England. Please tell the King that I shall not show the photograph to anybody. I love my husband, and he loves me. And he is a better man than the King. But here is a different photograph. And the King can keep this photograph if he likes.
>
> Irene Norton

"What a woman!" cried the King. "Why didn't I marry her? What a woman!"

"A very, very clever woman," said Sherlock Holmes coldly. "I am sorry, Your Majesty, that this business has not finished well."

"No, no," said the King. "She writes that she will never show the photograph to anybody. I need nothing

"I would like just one thing, Your Majesty. This photograph."

more than her word. There is no danger for me now. How can I thank you, dear Mr. Holmes?"

"I would like just one thing, Your Majesty."

"Tell me at once what it is," said the King.

"This photograph."

The King looked at him in surprise. "Irene's photograph?" he cried. "But of course. It is yours."

And so there was no terrible scandal in the royal families of Europe. And Sherlock Holmes still has the photograph of the woman who was cleverer than he was.

The Five Orange Pips

1

The Story of Uncle Elias

In September 1887 my wife was visiting some of her family, so I was staying with my old friend, Sherlock Holmes, in Baker Street. It was a windy, stormy evening, and the rain was falling heavily outside. Suddenly there was a knock at the door.

I looked at my friend in surprise. "Who can this be?" I asked.

"If he comes on business in this weather, it's important," said Sherlock Holmes. "Come in!" he called.

A young man came in. He looked wet, tired, and worried. "I've come to ask for help," he said. "I've heard of you, Mr. Holmes. People say you know everything. I don't know what to do."

"Well, sit down," said Holmes, "and tell me about yourself."

The young man sat down and put his wet feet near the fire. "My name is John Openshaw. My father, Joseph, had a brother, my uncle Elias, who went to live in America when he was young. He made a lot of money there. He didn't like the black Americans, so during the Civil War he fought *against* the men from the North and *with* those from the South. But when the South lost the war and there was equality for black people, Uncle Elias left America. So in 1869 he came back to England and went to live in a large house in the country. He was a strange, unhappy man.

"He did not want any friends," John Openshaw went on, "and he often drank a lot. But he liked me, and when I was twelve, I moved to Uncle Elias's house. He was very kind to me. I could go anywhere in the house. But there was one small room at the top of the house which was always locked. Nobody could go into this room.

"One day Uncle Elias got a letter from Pondicherry in India. 'I don't know anyone in Pondicherry!' he said, but when he opened the envelope, five little orange pips fell on to his plate. I began to laugh but stopped when I saw my uncle's white face.

" 'K.K.K.!' he cried. 'Oh my God, my God, they've found me!'

" 'What do you mean, uncle?' I asked.

" 'Death!' he cried, and he ran upstairs.

"I looked at the envelope, which had three Ks on the back. There was no letter. Who sent it? And why was my uncle so afraid?

"Uncle Elias went immediately to the secret room and took out a box which also had three Ks on it. He burned all the papers in the box and said to me, 'John, I know that I'm going to die soon. My brother, your father, will have all my money and my house after my death, and *you* will have it all when *he* dies. I hope you can enjoy it, but if not, give it to your worst enemy. I'm afraid that my money brings death with it.'

"I didn't understand what he meant, and nothing happened for a few weeks, so I did not feel so worried. But my uncle was very afraid. He stayed in his room most of the time and drank more than before. He always locked all the doors carefully. Then one night he drank very heavily and ran wildly out of the house, and in the morning we found him dead in a river. The police said he killed himself, but I knew he was afraid to die, so I didn't think that was true."

Holmes stopped the young man for a minute. "Tell me," he said. "When did your uncle get the letter from India, and when did he die?"

"The letter arrived on March 10th, 1883, and he died seven weeks later," answered John Openshaw.

"Thank you. Please go on," said Holmes.

"After my uncle's death, my father moved into the house. Of course I asked him to look carefully at the locked room, but we didn't find anything important."

2

More Pips

"Everything went well until a year later," said John Openshaw. "But one morning my father opened a letter to find five orange pips inside it. 'What does this mean, John?' he asked. His face was white.

"What does this mean, John?" my father asked.

" 'Look!' I said. 'There's K.K.K. on the envelope. Those letters were on Uncle Elias's envelope too!' We were both shaking and afraid.

" 'Yes, and this time it says "Put the papers in the garden." '

" 'Which papers? The papers in Uncle Elias's box? He burned them!' I said.

" 'And where has this letter come from?' my father said. He looked at the envelope. 'Dundee, Scotland. Well, I don't know anything about pips or papers. I'm not going to do anything.'

" 'Father, you have to tell the police,' I said.

"I remembered my uncle's letter from India, and I was very worried.

" 'No, they'll laugh at me. Let's just forget about it,' he replied.

"Three days later my poor father went to visit an old friend who lived some miles away. But he never came back. The police said that he was walking home in the dark when he fell down a hill. He was badly hurt, and he died soon after. They decided it was an accident, but I didn't agree. I thought it was murder, and I could not forget the five orange pips and the strange letters to my uncle and my father.

"But I've tried to forget, and I've lived alone in that house for nearly three years now. Then yesterday I got this."

The young man showed us an envelope with K.K.K.

on the back and five small orange pips. "You see?" he said. "It comes from East London, and it says 'Put the papers in the garden.' Those are the words that were in the letter to my father."

"So what did you do next?" asked Holmes.

"Nothing," answered Openshaw. He put his head in his hands. "I don't know what to do. I'm afraid."

"Nothing?" cried Holmes. "Young man, you must do something fast. You're in danger!"

"Well, I've talked to the police," said Openshaw unhappily. "But they laughed at me. They think that there's nothing to worry about."

"How stupid they are!" cried Holmes. "And why didn't you come to me immediately? Your enemies have had almost two days to make a plan. Haven't you found anything which will help us?"

"Well, I found this in the locked room," said John Openshaw. He showed us a small, half-burned piece of paper. "It was with my uncle's papers. It's his writing. Look, it says:

> March 7th, 1869 Sent the pips to three people, Brown, Robinson, and Williams.
> March 9th Brown left.
> March 10th Williams left.
> March 12th Visited Robinson and finished business with him.

"Thank you," said Sherlock Holmes. "And now you

must hurry home. Put this paper into your uncle's box, put in a letter which says that your uncle burned all the other papers, and put the box outside in the garden. I hope your enemies will be happy with that, and then you won't be in danger any more. How are you going home?"

"By train from Waterloo station," replied Openshaw.

"There'll be a lot of people in the streets, so I think that you'll be all right. But be careful."

"Thank you, Mr. Holmes," said Openshaw. "I'll do everything you say." He went out into the dark night, the wind and the rain.

3

K.K.K.

Sherlock Holmes sat silently and watched the fire. Then he said to me, "John Openshaw is in real danger. Why did his Uncle Elias have to leave America? Because he had enemies. When he came back to England, he was afraid. That's why he lived a lonely life and locked all his doors so carefully. Now where did those letters come from? Did you see?"

"The first from Pondicherry in India, the second from Dundee in Scotland, and the third from East London," I answered.

"Does that tell you anything?" asked Holmes.

Sherlock Holmes sat silently, and watched the fire.

"They're all sea ports. The writer was on a ship when he wrote the letters," I replied. I was pleased with my answer.

"Very good, Watson," said Holmes. "Somebody sent some pips from India and arrived seven weeks later to kill Uncle Elias. Then he sent some pips from Scotland and arrived three days later to kill John's father. Do you see why I'm worried now? He has sent pips to

John *from London*! John's enemy is in London already!"

"Good God, Holmes!" I cried. "Who is this man?"

"More than one man, I think. They belong to the Ku Klux Klan. That explains the 'K.K.K.' Haven't you ever heard of it? It's a very secret group of Americans from the South. They wanted to stop equality for black people and to kill anyone who didn't agree with them. The police couldn't stop them. But in 1869 Uncle Elias, who belonged to this secret group, suddenly left America with all their papers, and so the group could not go on. Of course the group wanted to get the papers back. You remember the half-burned paper? That was Uncle Elias's American diary. While he was working for the K.K.K., he sent the pips to frighten those three men. Two left the country, but one didn't, so the K.K.K. 'finished business with him', or killed him. The K.K.K. always worked like that."

"Well, I hope they won't kill young Openshaw," I said.

4

The Last Deaths

But they did. The next morning we read in the newspaper that John Openshaw was dead. A policeman found him in the river near Waterloo station. The police said it was an accident, but Holmes was very angry about it.

"He came to me for help, and those men murdered him! I'm going to find them if it's the last thing I do!" he said to me, and he hurried out of the house.

In the evening, when he came back to Baker Street, he was tired, but pleased. "Watson!" he said, "I know the names of Openshaw's enemies! And now I'm going to send them a surprise! This will frighten them!" He

We read in the newspaper that John Openshaw was dead.

took five pips from an orange and put them in an envelope. On it he wrote "S.H. for J.C."

"I'm sending the pips, not from the K.K.K., but from me, Sherlock Holmes, to Captain James Calhoun. His ship is called the *Star*. He and his men are sailing back to Georgia, in the USA, now."

"How did you find him, Holmes?" I asked.

"Ship's papers," he said. "I've looked at hundreds of them today. Only one ship, the *Star*, was in the three ports at the right times, and this morning the *Star* left London to sail back to Georgia. I found out that the captain and two of his men, all Americans, weren't on the ship last night, so I'm sure they killed poor John Openshaw. When they arrive in America, they'll get the pips and then the police will catch them!"

Sherlock Holmes is a very clever detective, but he can do nothing about the weather. The winter storms at sea that year were worse than ever, and so the *Star* never arrived in Georgia, and nobody saw the captain or his men again. The murderers of John Openshaw did not get the pips, but, in the end, death came to them.

GLOSSARY

air vent a hole, usually on an outside wall, to bring air into a room
band a thin, narrow piece of material to put around something (e.g., the neck or head)
bell rope a long piece of thin rope, fixed to a wall; you pull it to ring a bell
captain the most important person on a ship
civil war fighting between the people in one country
corridor a long narrow place in a house with doors which open into rooms
Count (*n*) a title ("Dr.", "Mrs.", "King" are titles) in front of a name
envelope you put a letter inside an envelope
equality when black people and white people can live and work together with no difficulty, there is equality
find out to ask questions and learn about something
fixed if something is fixed, it is not possible to move it
frighten to make someone afraid
God (**Good God, Oh my God, Thank God**) words which people say to show they are surprised, happy, thankful, etc.
gypsies wild people who don't live in houses, but travel around the country
hope (*v*) to want something to happen
king the most important man in a royal family
lawyer a person who helps someone with difficult business and keeps their important papers
majesty (**Your Majesty**) words that you say when you speak to a king or queen
mask (*n*) something to hide the face
metal something hard; gold, silver, steel, etc. are metals

pip a small white seed inside fruit like oranges
poison (*n*) something that will kill you or make you very ill if you eat or drink it
port a city or town by the sea where ships arrive or leave from
royal of a king or queen
scandal unkind talk about someone, which is bad for that person
servant someone who works in another person's house
snake a long thin animal without legs; many snakes are dangerous
speckled with small round marks of one color on top of another color
stepfather your mother's second husband (not your real father)
throw (past tense **threw**) to make something move through the air
uncle the brother of your father or mother
violent strong and dangerous
whistle (*n*) a high sound made not by the voice but by air through the lips
witness (*n*) somebody who sees something happen, and who writes their name to show that it really happened
worried (*adj*) afraid that something bad will happen

Sherlock Holmes Short Stories

ACTIVITIES

ACTIVITIES

Before Reading

1 How much do you know about detective stories? Think about these questions.

1 Have you read any stories about famous detectives? What are their names? Are they always policemen or policewomen?
2 Have you seen any films or television programs about detectives? Which ones? Which film or TV detective do you like best, and why?
3 In books or films, does the detective usually catch the criminal? Is the detective always "good" and the criminal always "bad"?

2 Read the story introduction on the first page of the book and the back cover. What do you know now, or what can you guess, about Sherlock Holmes? Check one of the boxes.

	YES	NO	MAYBE
1 He was a real person.	☐	☐	☐
2 He often worked with a friend.	☐	☐	☐
3 He always carried a gun.	☐	☐	☐
4 His apartment was in Baker Street.	☐	☐	☐
5 He worked in an office every day.	☐	☐	☐
6 He looked at people and things very carefully.	☐	☐	☐

ACTIVITIES

While Reading

The Speckled Band

Read Chapter 1, then answer these questions.

Who

1 . . . killed a servant?
2 . . . died in an accident eight years ago?
3 . . . died two years ago?
4 . . . was afraid of the wild animals and the gypsies?

Read Chapter 2. Here are some untrue sentences. Change them into true sentences.

1 Dr. Roylott did not need the girls' money.
2 Something was wrong with Helen's bedroom wall.
3 Helen and Julia often used the bell rope.
4 The air vent was outside the two bedrooms.

Before you read Chapter 3 (*Death in the Night*), can you guess what is going to happen?
Check one box each time.

	YES	NO
1 Dr. Roylott kills Helen.	☐	☐
2 Watson kills a cat.	☐	☐
3 Dr. Roylott dies.	☐	☐
4 Holmes finds the killer.	☐	☐
5 The gypsies kill Dr. Roylott.	☐	☐

A Scandal in Bohemia

Read Chapters 1 and 2. Are these sentences true (T) or false (F)?

1 Sherlock Holmes loved Irene Adler.
2 Watson and Holmes agreed to keep a secret.
3 Irene Adler had a photo of herself and the King.
4 Irene was happy to hear that the King was going to marry Clotilde.
5 The King gave Holmes two thousand pounds.
6 Holmes found out a lot from Irene Adler's servants.
7 Four taxis drove to the church of St. Monica.
8 Holmes helped Irene to marry Godfrey Norton.

Read Chapters 3 and 4. Choose the best question-word for these questions, and then answer them.

Who / Where / Why / What

1 . . . fell, with blood running down his face?
2 . . . did Irene bring Holmes into her house?
3 . . . did Watson throw the smoke stick into the room?
4 . . . happened next?
5 . . . did Irene hide the photo?
6 . . . said, "Good night, Mr. Sherlock Holmes"?
7 . . . was the King happy in the end?
8 . . . did Holmes ask the King to give him?

The Five Orange Pips

Read Chapters 1 and 2. Who said or wrote this?

1 "I've come to ask for help."
2 "I don't know anyone in Pondicherry!"
3 "He killed himself."
4 "Put the papers in the garden."
5 "Let's just forget about it."
6 "You must do something fast."
7 "Sent the pips to three people."
8 "I'll do everything you say."

Before you read Chapter 3 (*K. K. K.*) and Chapter 4 (*The Last Deaths*), can you guess the answers to these questions?

1 Are the K. K. K. Americans?
2 Where are the K. K. K. now?
3 Will they come to John Openshaw's house?
4 Will they kill John Openshaw?
5 Will Sherlock Holmes find the killers?
6 Will Sherlock Holmes need Dr. Watson's help?
7 How many people are going to die?
8 Will it be the end of the K. K. K?

ACTIVITIES

After Reading

1 **Look at these possible new titles for the three stories. Match all the titles with the stories. Which one do you like best for each story? Explain why.**

The Speckled Band

A Scandal in Bohemia

The Five Orange Pips

1 The King's Photograph
2 Death in an Envelope
3 Money Isn't Everything
4 A Dangerous Room
5 Finished Business
6 All for Love
7 Death in the Country
8 A Clever Woman
9 An Unexpected Death
10 A Dark Secret from the Past
11 Money Matters
12 In the Wrong Hands

2 **In *The Speckled Band*, perhaps the police asked one of the gypsies what he saw and heard on the night of Dr. Roylott's death. Use these words from the story to complete the conversation. (Use each word once.)**

anyone, bedroom, box, dead, friends, garden, happened, head, help, hours, light, listened, night, ran, saw, speckled, terrible, through, what, where, whistle, wife

POLICE: Tell me, where were you at midnight last _____?

GYPSY: I was outside in the _____, sitting around a small fire with my _____ and child, and some of our _____.

POLICE: Did you see _____ moving around in the garden?

GYPSY: Yes, I _____ two men. They crossed the garden and got into the house _____ Miss Stoner's _____ window.

POLICE: It was dark then. Were they carrying a _____?

GYPSY: No, but there was a light in the room, so they could see _____ to go.

POLICE: And what _____ next?

GYPSY: Nothing happened for about three _____. I waited near the house and _____. Then I heard a quiet _____, and after that a _____ cry from Dr. Roylott's room.

POLICE: Did you see _____ was happening in his room?

GYPSY: Yes, I _____ to his window and looked in. The two men were there. They were looking at a metal _____. And I saw Dr. Roylott sitting _____ in a chair, with a yellow _____ band around his _____. Then I ran away.

POLICE: Thank you for your _____. You can go now.

3 **Here is a conversation between the King of Bohemia and Irene Adler (see page 18 in *A Scandal in Bohemia*). The conversation is in the wrong order. Write it out in the correct order and put in the speakers' names. The King speaks first (number 3).**

1 _____ "Irene, please! You know that I cannot marry you. I must marry a woman of royal blood."

2 _____ "I think that I want to keep it. Perhaps I'll look at it every day and remember our love."

3 _____ "Irene, I've come to ask you for that photograph."

4 _____ "Don't talk about money! I'm not interested in that at all! Leave me alone! Leave this room at once!"

5 _____ "Think of my name and my family, Irene! There must be no scandal. I loved you, yes, I did, but that's finished now—"

6 _____ "Well, if I am not good enough for Your Majesty, no other woman will be. I'll send the photograph to Clotilde!"

7 _____ "But I must have it, Irene! If Clotilde von Saxe-Meningen ever sees that photograph—"

8 _____ "Finished? So, I'm like an old coat that you don't want to wear any more! What a fine friend you are!"

9 _____ "No! Irene, how much do you want for the photograph?"

10 _____ "Ah! If she sees it, perhaps she will not marry you! And there will be a scandal!"

4 In *The Five Orange Pips* perhaps Elias Openshaw kept a diary. Here is what he wrote at the end of March 10th, 1883. Use the linking words below to complete his diary for that day. (Use each word once.)

then / but / so / because / and / if / when / while / which / immediately / who

It's nighttime now, and I feel afraid, _____ I've locked all the doors very carefully. Today I received the five orange pips from the K. K. K.! I've been safe from them for the last fourteen years, _____ now I know that it's the end.

This morning I was at the breakfast table with young John _____ the servant brought in the mail delivery. There was a letter _____ came from Pondicherry in India. At first, I was surprised _____ I don't know anyone _____ lives there. _____ I realized that it meant death! The five orange pips were in the envelope, _____ they fell on to my plate.

_____, I hurried upstairs to fetch the K. K. K. box from the locked room. _____ John was watching, I burned all the papers in the box. But it's no good, I know that they will find me and kill me! And _____ poor John gets my money one day, he will die too!

5 What do you think about Sherlock Holmes and Dr. Watson? Think about these questions.

1 Do you think Sherlock Holmes is a clever detective? What is he especially good at?
2 Why do people ask Holmes for help? Does he always keep them out of danger?
3 What do you think about Dr. Watson? Is he as clever as Holmes? Does Holmes really need him?
4 Is Holmes ready to kill someone who has killed another person (like Dr. Roylott)? Is Holmes himself a killer?
5 Does Holmes always find the answer? Is he always cleverer than the other people in the stories?

6 Which story did you like best, and which did you like least? Can you explain why? Write a short review of one of the stories. Use these words to help you.

I liked / didn't like this story because . . .
. . . nobody died
. . . could / couldn't guess the answer
. . . the murderer(s) was (were) killed
. . . a good person was murdered
. . . somebody was cleverer than Sherlock Holmes
. . . happy / unhappy ending

ABOUT THE AUTHOR

Sir Arthur Conan Doyle (1859—1930) was born in Edinburgh, Scotland. He studied medicine and worked as a doctor for eight years. Because he wanted to earn more money, he started writing, and soon people were reading his stories in weekly magazines.

In the opening pages of his first novel, *A Study in Scarlet* (1887), Sherlock Holmes appeared for the first time—a strange, coldly intelligent detective, who smokes a pipe, plays the violin, and lives at 221B Baker Street in London. He can find the answer to almost any problem and often explains how easy it is to his slow-thinking friend, Dr. Watson ("Elementary, my dear Watson!"). Readers began to show great interest in Holmes when *The Sign of Four* was published in 1890, and short stories about him in the *Strand* magazine, were very popular.

Conan Doyle himself preferred writing novels about history like *The White Company* (1891), and he soon became bored with the Sherlock Holmes character. So, in *The Final Problem* (1893) he "killed" him, when Holmes and his famous enemy, Moriarty, fell to their deaths in the Reichenbach falls. But because people wanted more stories about Holmes, Conan Doyle had to bring him back to life, in *The Hound of the Baskervilles* (1902) and many more stories.

You can read Sherlock Holmes stories in almost any language, and there are many plays and films about the great detective.

OXFORD BOOKWORMS LIBRARY

Classics • Crime & Mystery • Factfiles • Fantasy & Horror
Human Interest • Playscripts • Thriller & Adventure
True Stories • World Stories

The OXFORD BOOKWORMS LIBRARY provides enjoyable reading in English, with a wide range of classic and modern fiction, non-fiction, and plays. It includes original and adapted texts in seven carefully graded language stages which take learners from beginner to advanced level.

All Stage 1 titles, as well as over eighty other titles from Starter to Stage 6, are available as audio recordings. All Starters and many titles at Stages 1 to 4 are specially recommended for younger learners. Every Bookworm is illustrated, and Starters and Factfiles have full-color illustrations.

The OXFORD BOOKWORMS LIBRARY also offers extensive support. Each book contains an introduction to the story, notes about the author, a glossary, and activities. Additional resources include tests and worksheets, as well as answers for these and for the activities in the books. There is advice on running a class library, using audio recordings, and the many ways of using Oxford Bookworms in reading programs. Resource materials are available on the website <www.oup.com/bookworms>.

The *Oxford Bookworms Collection* is a series for advanced learners. It consists of volumes of short stories by well-known authors, both classic and modern. Texts are not abridged or adapted in any way, but carefully selected to be accessible to the advanced student.

You can find details and a full list of titles in the *Oxford Bookworms Library Catalog* and *Oxford English Language Teaching Catalogs*, and on the website <www.oup.com/bookworms>.

BOOKWORMS · FANTASY & HORROR · STAGE 2

Dracula

BRAM STOKER

Retold by Diane Mowat

In the mountains of Transylvania there stands a castle. It is the home of Count Dracula—a dark, lonely place. At night the wolves howl around the walls …

In the year 1875 Jonathan Harker comes from England to do business with the Count. But Jonathan does not feel comfortable at Castle Dracula. Strange things happen at night, and very soon he begins to feel afraid. And he is right to be afraid because Count Dracula is one of the Un-Dead—a vampire that drinks the blood of living people …

BOOKWORMS · CLASSICS · STAGE 2

Robinson Crusoe

DANIEL DEFOE

Retold by Diane Mowat

"I often walked along the shore, and one day I saw something in the sand. I went over to look at it more carefully … It was a footprint—the footprint of a man!"

In 1659 Robinson Crusoe was shipwrecked on a small island off the coast of South America. After fifteen years alone, he suddenly learns that there is another person on the island. But will this man be a friend—or an enemy?

BOOKWORMS · HUMAN INTEREST · STAGE 2

New Yorkers

O. HENRY

Retold by Diane Mowat

A housewife, a tramp, a lawyer, a waitress, an actress—ordinary people living ordinary lives in New York at the beginning of this century. The city has changed greatly since that time, but its people are much the same. Some are rich, some are poor, some are happy, some are sad, some have found love, and some are looking for love.

O. Henry's famous short stories—sensitive, funny, sympathetic—give us vivid pictures of the everyday lives of these New Yorkers.

BOOKWORMS · CLASSICS · STAGE 2

Huckleberry Finn

MARK TWAIN

Retold by Diane Mowat

Who wants to live in a house, wear clean clothes, be good, and go to school every day? Not young Huckleberry Finn, that's for sure. So Huck runs away and is soon floating down the great Mississippi River on a raft. With him is Jim, a black slave who is also running away. But life is not always easy for the two friends.

And there's 300 dollars waiting for anyone who catches poor Jim ...

BOOKWORMS · FANTASY & HORROR · STAGE 3

Frankenstein

MARY SHELLEY

Retold by Patrick Nobes

Victor Frankenstein thinks he has found the secret of life. He takes parts from dead people and builds a new "man." But this monster is so big and frightening that everyone runs away from him—even Frankenstein himself!

The monster is like an enormous baby who needs love. But nobody gives him love, and soon he learns to hate. And, because he is so strong, the next thing he learns is how to kill ...

BOOKWORMS · CLASSICS · STAGE 3

The Call of the Wild

JACK LONDON

Retold by Nick Bullard

When men find gold in the frozen north of Canada, they need dogs—big, strong dogs to pull the sleds on the long journeys to and from the gold mines.

Buck is stolen from his home in the south and sold as a sled-dog. He has to learn a new way of life—how to work in harness, how to stay alive in the ice and the snow ... and how to fight. Because when a dog falls down in a fight, he never gets up again.